Queen LATIFAH

Biography

Queen LATIFAH

Amy Ruth

A&E

Lerner Publications Company
Minneapolis

For my husband, who always
makes me feel like a queen

Copyright © 2001 by Lerner Publications Company

Lerner Publications Company
A division of Lerner Publishing Group
241 First Avenue North
Minneapolis, MN 55401 U.S.A.

Website address: www.lernerbooks.com

Library of Congress Cataloging-in-Publication Data

Ruth, Amy.
    Queen Latifah / by Amy Ruth.
        p.   cm. — (A&E biography)
    Includes discography, filmography, and index.
    Summary: A biography of the young woman who rose from humble beginnings in New Jersey to become a popular rap singer, actress, and role model.
    ISBN 0-8225-4988-3 (lib. bdg. : alk. paper)
    1. Latifah, Queen—Juvenile literature. 2. Rap musicians—United States—Biography—Juvenile literature. [1. Latifah, Queen. 2. Rap musicians. 3. Afro-Americans—Biography. 4. Women—Biography.]
I. Title. II. Series.
ML3930.L178 R98 2001
782.421649'092—dc21   99-050945

Manufactured in the United States of America
1 2 3 4 5 6 – JR – 06 05 04 03 02 01

CONTENTS

As a teenager in the mid-1980s, Dana Owens (later known as Queen Latifah) danced at the Latin Quarter nightclub in New York City. The club has been popular since the 1950s.

Chapter **ONE**

DANA

NEW YORK CITY'S LATIN QUARTER NIGHTCLUB shook with music and people. It was the mid-1980s, and the beat of an exciting new musical style, called rap, throbbed throughout the Times Square club district. Hundreds of people stood outside the Latin Quarter anxiously waiting to go inside. On the dance floor, throngs of people—including Dana Owens, a teenager from nearby East Orange, New Jersey— danced to the pulsating beat and chanted along with the disc jockeys. Onstage, rappers threw out their rhymes over the music from records spinning on turntables.

To Dana, rap was more than just entertainment. With its immense sound and profound lyrics, rap was pure drama. This new music was so powerful that Dana broke her curfew to experience it. After her mother and brother were asleep, she sneaked out of their apartment to join her friends for a night of club hopping. Sometimes she took the subway into Manhattan. Other times she rode with a friend who had a car. It didn't matter how Dana got to the clubs—only that she was there and part of the scene.

"Immediately I was one with this world," she said later. "My blood beat to its beat. Not only did I want to be there, I *had* to be there, and nothing was going to stop me. Not even breaking my mother's heart."

Just a few years later, Dana Owens, barely out of high school, became rap music's ruling female superstar, Queen Latifah. Armed with positive messages about black unity, racial harmony, self-respect, and the empowerment of women, Queen Latifah added a fresh dimension to the male-dominated, often vulgar and violent world of rap music. While still a teen, she established the standards that future female rappers would follow.

Queen Latifah was the first female solo rapper to sign with a major record label, and she soon became the first to score a gold record. But this was only the beginning for the Queen, who is a talented actor and a savvy businessperson. In just over a decade, she recorded four albums, made eleven movies, starred in a top-rated television series, and premiered her own talk show.

Queen Latifah's positive style of rapping—without the sexism and violence of many rappers—caught on quickly with music fans.

It didn't take long for Latifah to become a role model for young people around the world. Music critics, politicians, and other social commentators praised the Queen's stand against violence and sexism in rap lyrics, calling her "a leading voice of her generation."

Dana Elaine Owens was born on March 17, 1970, in Newark, New Jersey. Her parents, Rita Bray Owens and Lancelot Owens, welcomed their first daughter with relief—Dana was born almost one month late, and they had grown anxious waiting for her.

"From the very beginning, I knew my daughter was going to be different," said Mrs. Owens. "Dana refused to be born. Ten long months I carried her. I finally had to tell the doctors to go in and get her. And she fought that, too."

Dana's brother, Lancelot Jr., was two years older than Dana. He was known by his nickname, Winki, because as a baby he looked like he was winking.

The Owens family lived in an apartment in Newark, an industrial city in eastern New Jersey, where Dana's father was a police officer. As Mr. Owens advanced in his career, the family moved several times to nicer apartments in better neighborhoods.

Mrs. Owens was a talented artist, and she and her husband shared a love of music. From the time Dana was a little girl, she loved to sing. She and Winki enjoyed giving impromptu song and dance performances for their parents. Performing seemed to be second nature to Dana.

Rita Owens recalled, "Give her a pot, she'd bang it. A spoon, she'd sing into it. A box, she'd beat it."

It was music that had brought Dana's parents together. Rita Bray's father was an army sergeant stationed on a base in Arlington, Virginia. Lancelot Owens, a soldier in the Honor Guard, was stationed there at the same time. When he was off duty, Lance sang with his musical group, the Grand Prix Machine, in the service club on the base. One afternoon, sixteen-year-old Rita Bray and her sister Angela, nicknamed Angel, came to the club and auditioned to be backup singers for the band. Soon after they met, Lancelot asked Rita to marry him. The newlyweds settled in Newark, where Lance had grown up.

Latifah once said her parents worked together like

musical harmony, their individual strengths complementing each other. And Mr. and Mrs. Owens made a point of treating Dana and Winki equally, a parenting style that was progressive for the time. In the 1970s, Americans were just beginning to view women as equals in the workplace, the sports arena, and the classroom. Determined that their daughter would not grow up thinking girls couldn't do certain things, Dana's parents equipped her with self confidence and determination.

Mrs. Owens encouraged Dana to believe in herself and her dreams. And she taught both her children the importance of open, honest communication. "I wanted Dana to feel that there was nothing she couldn't talk to me about," said her mother. "And there wasn't. [I gave] my son and daughter a healthy amount of freedom and encouraged them to question me so that we could have a dialogue."

Mr. Owens taught Dana to be physically strong and to take care of herself. "I'm not afraid of too many things," Latifah told a reporter in 1993. "And I got that invincible kind of attitude from [my father]."

A martial arts expert, Mr. Owens enrolled his children in a Newark karate studio. Although Mrs. Owens didn't like the idea of Dana learning the sport, she did not share her feelings with her daughter.

"I was afraid she would get hurt," Mrs. Owens said. "But I never stopped her. I was mindful not to interfere with her desires—no matter how unconventional they may have been."

With her parents' constant encouragement and support, Dana's strong and lively personality continued to blossom. And with each challenge she met, her confidence soared. Her mother once described her as a dynamo. Mr. and Mrs. Owens discovered early that their little dynamo could take care of herself.

When Dana was in kindergarten, a teacher accidentally locked her out of the school building. Dana and her classmates had been waiting on the playground just as they always did. But when it was time to line up and go inside, Dana was separated from her classmates. She found herself alone on the playground, with no way into the locked school building. Knowing that her Grandmother Owens lived nearby, five-year-old Dana set out for her house. Following the route she knew only from car trips with her parents, Dana safely crossed several major streets. A mile and a half later, she was knocking on her grandmother's door.

Even though she was a strong and independent child, Dana still needed the comfort of friends and family. From the time she was born, Dana was close to her brother. Dana and Winki both enjoyed the outdoors. Dana loved to climb trees and ride her bike. She often joined Winki and his friends in their roughhousing and chasing games.

When she fell and cut her knees or bruised herself playing basketball, Dana proudly showed off her scrapes. "Those 'marks' were the mark of a girl unafraid," Latifah later said.

Sometimes other girls in the neighborhood teased her by calling her a tomboy. Dana replied that she was not a tomboy but an athlete.

Mr. Owens, who had fought in the Vietnam War and learned to survive in the wild, wanted his children to understand the forces of nature. He took Dana and Winki on walks and camping trips, showing them how to identify plants, find insects, and start a campfire safely.

When Dana was six, Mr. Owens took her and Winki on their first camping trip. Rain drummed down steadily all weekend. Refusing to go home, Mr. Owens instead transformed the disappointment into a learning opportunity, telling the children: "Hey, life's not always going to be sunshine every day. What are you going to do when there are a few clouds? You have to keep going." By the end of the trip, Dana was exhilarated by a sense of accomplishment.

Education was also important in the Owens household, and Dana and Winki attended private schools. Their parents believed these schools reinforced the lessons the children learned at home—hard work, discipline, and self-respect.

Learning was also a part of the family's recreational time. Mrs. Owens brought books along on picnics and visits to the park to teach her children about science, math, and nature. Proud of their heritage, Mr. and Mrs. Owens taught their children to respect their African roots and culture. Dana and Winki learned

African Queens

From the time she was a young girl, Dana was fascinated with the powerful women who governed kingdoms in ancient Africa. Egypt, where pharaohs once ruled as gods, is perhaps the best-known African kingdom. Queens Cleopatra, Tiye, and Nefertiti governed Egypt at different times in its history. Queen Hapshepsut, Egypt's first female ruler, sat on the throne for three decades and was the first woman to be buried in the Valley of the Kings.

During the sixteenth century, Queen Nzingha ruled over the Ndongo people in southern Africa. A clever politician, Nzingha formed several military alliances that kept her subjects safe from Portuguese slave traders for thirty years. In the same century, Queen Amina ruled the West African province of Zazzau for thirty-four years. Known as "the woman as capable as a man," she expanded the kingdom more than any other ruler in Zazzau's history.

Many African queens are remembered for their strength and courage. Queen Candance of Sudan led her armies into battle against the Roman ruler Caesar Augustus. In the kingdom of Ghana, Queen Yaa Asantewa led the Ashanti people into battle against English colonists, just as Queen Dahia Al-Kahina had led her soldiers against Arab invaders around 690 B.C.

Queen Nefertiti

Under the leadership of female rulers, some of the world's first civilizations flourished and endured. Stories of African queens' bravery, intelligence, and beauty passed from generation to generation as part of Africa's oral traditions. Hundreds of years after these queens lived, their descendants honored them by recording their stories in writing.

that they were descendants of African royalty. Dana was especially fascinated by the African queens who proudly ruled their nations.

This focus on learning paid off. Officials at Dana's school identified her as gifted and talented, and she was able to skip a grade.

For Dana and Winki, early childhood was a happy time. Latifah once compared her family to television's Huxtable family, made famous in the 1980s program *The Cosby Show*. There were plenty of hugs and daily doses of praise and encouragement in the Owens household. When Mr. Owens came home from work, and on his days off, he loved roughhousing with his kids. The house rang with the sounds of jazz, rock and roll, and soul music. On Sundays the family attended church, where Dana fell in love with the rich sounds of gospel music.

"We had a lot of love and laughter in our house," Latifah said. "We had a lot of jokes and a lot of quality time. . . . My brother and I didn't have a care in the world."

Members of the U.S. National Guard patrol an African American neighborhood in Newark, New Jersey, in 1967. Riots in the 1960s left Dana's hometown weakened economically.

Chapter **TWO**

LATIFAH

THE YEAR **1978** BROUGHT TWO MAJOR CHANGES TO Dana's carefree life. The first was a new name—Latifah, a Muslim name. In the 1970s, many African Americans took Muslim names as a symbol of their determination to overcome social injustices and to establish black pride.

With the Civil Rights movement of the 1950s and 1960s, black citizens had succeeded in changing the nation's laws to end legal discrimination. But those laws did not ensure good jobs, decent health care, quality education, and affordable housing for all citizens. The United States continued to be racially segrgated in many ways. The majority of African Americans earned a living by working in low-paying jobs.

BLACK MOVEMENTS OF THE 1960s AND 1970s

Several political and social movements grew out of the Civil Rights movement and gained momentum in the turbulent 1960s and 1970s. Although all of these movements encouraged black independence and cultural pride, conflicting ideas reflected disagreement among black Americans about how to achieve their goals.

Some activists, like civil rights leader Martin Luther King Jr. and his followers, envisioned an integrated nation and harmony across racial lines. The Civil Rights movement embraced nonviolence as a response to widespread police brutality. Leaders of the Nation of Islam, a religious movement founded in 1930, articulated black citizens' right to defend themselves.

The Nation of Islam was based on the Near and Middle Eastern religion of Islam. Followers of Islam, called Muslims, worship Allah as god and revere the prophet Muhammad. For blacks in the United States, the Nation of Islam offered positive alternatives to unemployment, hopelessness, and crime. Black Muslim leaders, including the well-known Malcolm X, inspired many people with their message of black superiority.

Still another group of black nationalists emerged. Founded in California in 1966, the Black Panther Party for Self-Defense demanded an equal society. Like black Muslims, the Black Panthers supported violence in response to police brutality in their communities. The party set up civic organizations, free health clinics, and school lunch programs, reflecting the widely held belief that blacks should invest in their own communities. Within a year of the party's founding, the militant Black Panthers were recognized by their black leather jackets and black berets. They had established chapters in twenty-five cities nationwide.

In 1966 Stokely Carmichael, once a persuasive, nonviolent civil rights activist, began a more aggressive campaign for civil rights. At a rally in Mississippi, he called for "Black Power," a phrase that panicked many white citizens. Carmichael eventually joined the Black Panthers, who popularized the controversial Black Power salute—a clenched fist raised to the sky.

Like many religious, cultural, and political movements, the African American–led movements of the 1960s and 1970s experienced internal conflicts. In 1964 Malcolm X left the Nation of Islam and founded Muslim Mosque, Inc. A year later, he was assassinated. Many people believe he was killed because some of his ideas conflicted with black Muslim beliefs.

Black Panther members grew apart, separated by differing visions for the organization. Some wanted the group to continue its militant activism, while others believed the party should emphasize its community service programs. By the end of the 1970s, the Black Panther Party barely existed.

The Civil Rights movement also splintered into different groups. In the late 1960s, younger civil rights activists lost their faith in

the peaceful protest ideas of Dr. Martin Luther King Jr., who was assassinated in April 1968. Many people who had fought for civil rights joined the Black Panthers or got involved in other Black Power activities. Some African Americans left the United States to settle in Africa.

Dr. Martin Luther King Jr., left, and Malcolm X, right, were key leaders in the Civil Rights movement.

Many lived in poor, run-down neighborhoods. Black workers in professional positions found themselves performing the same duties as their white counterparts, but for lower wages. Without sympathetic politicians representing African Americans in local, state, and national government, conditions would not improve. In urban areas, crime, hopelessness, and unemployment mounted.

For black youths, these social, economic, and political conditions added up to a bleak future. Frustrated and angry, black people in large urban areas, including Los Angeles, Minneapolis, Detroit, and Newark, protested in the late 1960s by rioting. The riots usually began after an incident or a rumor of police brutality. Black youths and adults filled the streets, looting and burning stores and homes. The rioters wanted their white neighbors and lawmakers to know that they were fed up with second-class social and economic status.

Following the riots, black Americans looked for a way to rebuild their broken communities. Many turned to the Nation of Islam, founded in Detroit, Michigan, in 1930. This religious movement provided a spiritual and cultural community for African Americans, who were encouraged to take pride in themselves and their communities. Another way people demonstrated their pride was by taking a Muslim name to replace their European American names, which were often described as "slave names."

Many of Dana's black friends assumed Muslim

names. Winki took the name Jameel, which means "beautiful." But eight-year-old Dana hadn't considered taking a Muslim name for herself until her cousin Sharonda Mamoud, who was a Muslim, suggested it. One day when the two girls were hanging out, Sharonda excitedly showed Dana a book that listed Muslim names and their meanings. Sharonda had chosen the name Salima Wadiah, meaning "safe and healthy." Dana carefully looked through the pages of names, wanting to find a perfect fit.

"I knew then that something as simple as picking a new name for myself would be my first act of defining who I was—for myself and for the world," Latifah recalled in her autobiography.

When she came to the name *Latifah*, Dana said it out loud, getting the feel of the letters rolling off her tongue. She liked how the name sounded, but even more than that, she liked what it meant: sensitive, kind, and delicate.

"The name accurately described exactly who I was inside," remembered Latifah, who was mostly known as Dana until she started rapping professionally. "I loved how it made me feel—feminine and special. The people in my world may have perceived me as something else, but . . . I knew who I was inside and I wanted to show a bit of that on the outside."

Dana's selection of the name Latifah confirmed what Mrs. Owens had always known about her daughter who loved sports and hated dresses. "Dana's daintiness was internal," her mother said. "She had softness and gentleness. They were very much a part of my daughter's character. If you told Dana she had disappointed you, she would shed tears. She was, above all, sensitive. My daughter was strong on the outside, but soft as a down pillow on the inside."

It was precisely Dana's sensitivity that made it hard for her to cope with the next major event of 1978— her parents' separation. Family had always been important to Dana's parents, who both came from large families. Sadly, though, family ties were not enough to help Mr. Owens overcome his personal problems. During his career as a soldier and police officer, Mr. Owens had killed several people in the line of duty, but he had difficulty coming to terms with the taking of human life. He did not get psychological counseling for his troubles and was unable to deal with them on his own. Haunted by painful memories, Mr. Owens became depressed, and by 1978, he had developed a dangerous cocaine addiction.

A drug that affects the central nervous system, cocaine provides temporary pleasure. But it places stress on vital organs, such as the heart and lungs, and eventually poisons the body. When the high wears off, the user craves more of the drug and may become paranoid and violent. In the 1970s, cocaine use was on the rise, and the drug's dangers were becoming well known. To keep her children safe, Mrs. Owens made the difficult decision to leave the man she loved.

"We could not imagine that we would no longer be a family," Latifah remembered. "I couldn't understand what was happening. I just knew we were leaving."

Although Dana and Winki both struggled with the painful news, Dana especially suffered from the breakup of her family. For a time, her happy, confident personality was overshadowed by sadness, anger, and doubt. Though her parents had taught her the importance of communication, she had trouble expressing her emotions. "Dana became very aggressive and very defiant," Mrs. Owens said. "She wasn't able to vocalize her hurt until much later."

The Owens family lived for two years in a housing development in Newark, New Jersey, similar to the one shown above. The "projects," as they were called, housed several thousand low-income residents.

Chapter **THREE**

HYATT COURT

THE OWENSES' SEPARATION BROUGHT IMMEDIATE changes. Mrs. Owens, Dana, and Winki moved out of the family's apartment. For a while, they lived in a pretty garden apartment in a nice neighborhood in Newark. But without Mr. Owens's financial support, money was in short supply. Mrs. Owens had no choice but to move Dana and Winki into Hyatt Court, a government-subsidized housing development in East Newark. She promised that the move to "the projects" was only temporary, and Dana tried not to get discouraged.

Still, Dana couldn't help but remember the times her family would pile into the car and drive around Newark's upscale neighborhoods. They imagined what it would be like to live in a fancy mansion. Inspecting her new surroundings, Dana knew she was farther from those mansions than she had ever been.

"Until then, our family had always been moving to a better place and a better neighborhood," Latifah said. "But this time, it wasn't a step up."

Hyatt Court was a group of three brick apartment buildings situated around a courtyard, which served as the facility's social gathering place. Residents—many unemployed or on welfare—sat on their stoops overlooking the courtyard. There was almost always music playing from a portable radio. Kids hung out and pets roamed the grounds.

The Owens family moved into an apartment on the third floor. Although Hyatt Court was a temporary stop on the way to a better place, Mrs. Owens quickly transformed the apartment into a home.

"My mother wanted 3K to feel like our space," Latifah wrote later. "With so much change in our young lives, she knew just how extra important it was for us to feel comfortable and safe."

Dana and Winki each had their own room. Dana's was a place where she could be alone with her thoughts and imagination. She arranged the furniture to create an open area where she could dance to her favorite music, including the Jackson 5, the Delfonics, and Jamaican reggae music. Listening to the familiar tunes of her favorite performers helped her adjust to her new home.

While Dana was coping with the changes in her life, the world around her was also changing. In the 1970s, people of all races and backgrounds voiced their concerns about a variety of issues, such as the environment and racial and gender discrimination. Music became an important form of expression during these turbulent times. Many singer-songwriters, white and black, sang about personal, political, and social issues.

The Owenses' apartment was a bright spot in a housing complex Latifah once described as a barren landscape. The walls, steps, and hallways of Hyatt Court were often littered with garbage. Graffiti was scrawled across walls outside and inside. Heated arguments could be heard in the hallways.

Mrs. Owens continued to send her children to private school, even though the tuition was sometimes a financial hardship for her. "Just because you're living in the projects, doesn't mean you're *of* the projects," Mrs. Owens told her kids.

Dana and Winki were anxious to leave Hyatt Court, and Mrs. Owens worked hard to make that happen. She was determined to buy a house, and she held several jobs to earn the necessary down payment. At night, she worked at the Newark post office. When her shift ended at 7:00 A.M., she headed home to get Dana and Winki off to school before going to her waitressing job at the Newark airport. Despite their mother's busy schedule, Dana and Winki never had to come home to an empty apartment after school.

NEWARK

nce a thriving city, Newark was changed forever in 1967. On the night of July 12, white police officers stopped a black cabdriver for a minor traffic violation. Across the street from a Newark police station, black residents of an apartment complex watched as police officers dragged the cabdriver inside. Soon rumors spread that police had beaten the cabdriver to death, and an angry mob gathered. Rioters spilled into the streets, smashing windows, looting stores, and burning entire city blocks to the ground.

By the third night of rioting, National Guard soldiers arrived in Newark, the first of six thousand troops. (National Guard soldiers are assigned to a certain region, state, or city. They are trained to respond quickly to state and local emergencies.) After five days, the rioting stopped. About fifteen hundred black citizens had been arrested, and twenty-six people were dead. Twenty-four of the victims were black. Investigators later concluded that panicky soldiers had killed many innocent bystanders.

In the years following the riots, many white middle-class residents left Newark. They took with them their tax dollars, which had helped pay for schools and other public services. State and U.S. lawmakers tried to help redevelop the city. And in 1970, Newark residents elected the city's first black mayor, Kenneth Gibson, who served until 1986. Nonetheless, progress and reforms came slowly. Newark's crime rate and unemployment remained high.

By the time Dana moved to Hyatt Court in 1978, Newark had lost 20 percent of its population in just two decades. Like Hyatt Court, Newark's landscape was barren.

Before Mrs. Owens married Dana's father, she had planned to attend college. She had been accepted at Howard University in Washington, D.C., and at Spelman College in Atlanta, Georgia. But she postponed college to be a wife and mother. After she separated from her husband, Mrs. Owens revived her dream of becoming a trained artist. She enrolled in Kean University, near Newark. Taking classes part time, she studied to become an art teacher. Dana and Winki often accompanied their mother to campus.

When they weren't at school, Dana and Winki avoided the Hyatt Court courtyard and the kids who hung out there. Without friends in the neighborhood, brother and sister grew even closer.

When school let out for the summer, Hyatt Court exploded with the sounds and activities of restless young people. The sun beat down on the city, trapping the heat in the concrete streets, sidewalks, and buildings. But the rising temperatures didn't keep kids from crowding into the Hyatt Court courtyard, looking for something to do. Sometimes they spent entire days just hanging around, not doing anything. Many got into trouble selling drugs in the surrounding streets.

To keep Dana and Winki out of this environment, Mrs. Owens sent them to visit her family in Virginia. There, the long, sultry summer days were filled with family, wholesome fun, and a sense of quiet that Newark could not offer. Grandma Bray's yard had trees for Dana and Winki to climb and large open spaces for them to play in. Dana loved being out in nature, something she rarely found in her urban New Jersey home. She enjoyed breathing the clean air, watching the birds, and feeling the soft grass tickle her bare feet.

"There our life slowed down," Latifah remembered. "We ate from fruit bushes and pecan trees. There were [swimming] pools with clean water where there weren't a thousand kids crammed in like at Newark's pools. People smiled and had manners."

Vacations in Virginia provided something else Dana loved—a built-in audience. Mrs. Owens came from a family of seven children, so Dana and Winki had plenty of aunts, uncles, and cousins. Dana had fun performing and showing off her musical and theatrical skills. And she delighted her relatives with her natural talent for mimicking people she heard on television and radio. She especially enjoyed doing accents and perfected her Jamaican, French, and Spanish imitations.

"She liked to be in the spotlight, where people would look at her and laugh," Dana's grandmother, Katherine Bray, remembered.

Dana's Aunt Angel was impressed with her niece's talent and tenacity. "She was the go-getter," she said. "She always aspired to do, and she did."

Although Mrs. Owens worked hard to create a good life for her children, there was still a void. Dana and Winki missed their "Pops." While Mr. Owens struggled to overcome his drug dependence, he maintained a relationship with his children. Dana and Winki enjoyed the times when their father treated them to a Chinese dinner and led them in karate exercises. Although Dana and Winki saw much less of their father after the separation, they knew he loved them.

"He was always around," Latifah said. "He was never far. I could always reach him."

After two years in Hyatt Court, Mrs. Owens had saved enough money for a down payment on a house. She took Dana and Winki house-hunting, and the three fell in love with a light blue home with a small yard. In the early 1980s, however, most banks would not loan money to divorced women or to women who did not have a credit history that proved they had already borrowed money and successfully repaid it. Banks also discriminated against minorities. When Mrs. Owens tried to secure a bank loan to buy the small blue house for her family, she was denied.

Determined to keep her promise to leave Hyatt Court, Mrs. Owens rented a house on Littleton Avenue, in an attractive section of Newark. Dana loved the large, airy rooms in her new home. But the best feature by far was the big backyard. After two years in Hyatt Court, Dana was back to playing kickball and basketball in a safe, quiet neighborhood. She regained the feelings of security and progress that had been lost when she moved to Hyatt Court.

Dana was well liked even before she became well known. In high school, she was voted Most Popular, Most Comical, Best All Around, and Best Dancer.

Chapter **FOUR**

B-Girl

DANA STOOD NERVOUSLY BEHIND THE STAGE IN THE St. Anne's School auditorium. The seventh grader had landed the leading role of Dorothy in the musical *The Wiz*. She was about to make her stage debut to an auditorium packed with classmates, teachers, friends, and parents. In the audience, Mrs. Owens, Winki, and other family members waited anxiously for the curtain to rise and Dana to step onto the stage.

For the rest of the evening, Dana moved the audience with her strong, clear voice. When she sang the song "Home," the audience gave her a standing ovation. Mrs. Owens and Winki were astonished. They knew Dana loved singing, but they had not realized the extent of her abilities.

"I had never heard her sing like that before," Mrs. Owens remembered. "People were crying."

In 1984 Dana made the leap from the St. Anne's stage to the larger auditorium at Irvington High School. Dana was already familiar with her new school. After Mrs. Owens graduated from college, she had been hired as an art teacher at Irvington.

Around the same time, the family moved to an apartment on Halsted Street in East Orange, a small city bordering Newark. Despite her outgoing personality, Dana always felt a little insecure when she moved to a new neighborhood. But she perked up immediately when she met Mondo, a high school senior who became her first boyfriend. Mondo treated Dana with respect, and she liked that. As she had matured, Dana had learned about the troubles in her parents' marriage. She was shocked to discover that Mr. Owens had fathered three other children in addition to her and Winki. The news left Dana feeling confused and vulnerable, but Mondo helped her sort through her doubts about relationships. Not long after they met, Mondo left for college, but they kept in touch.

When she transferred to Irvington as a sophomore in 1984, Dana lost no time entering the student talent contests. Singing "If Only For One Night," a love song by Luther Vandross, Dana won the Irvington High School Talent Show that year. A big fan of reggae, the Jackson 5, and Patti LaBelle, Dana seemed to be singing all the time.

At Irvington High School, Dana won student talent contests.

Dana loved Irvington High. She was a good student and also excelled on the basketball court. After high school, she hoped to earn a broadcast journalism degree and maybe even become a lawyer. She enjoyed debating with her friends about racism, drugs, and apartheid—the South African government's policy of racial segregation. A poet at heart, Dana loved writing and reading poems. In black poet and activist Nikki Giovanni, she found a strong voice much like her own.

"Nikki's poems struck me. I could feel her," Dana said. "I liked her play on words and how she threw a little rhythm around. All her poetry seemed to be real and to have love in it. It was based on the fact that she cared about herself and about black people."

Dana was a star basketball player at Irvington High. Her skills helped her team win the state title in her sophomore year.

The same year Dana cleaned up at the school talent show, the girls' basketball team stomped its competitors all the way to the state championship game. Playing in the forward position, Dana helped her team win the state title that year.

Tammy Hammond, a fellow basketball star, became Dana's best friend. The two hung out together at Tammy's house, which overflowed with activity.

Dana's self-assuredness made her influential with her peers. Her high standards often rubbed off on those around her. For example, she learned that a boy named Shakim Compere, who was in her geometry class, had a crush on her. She explained to him that she couldn't date him because he had several bad habits, including smoking and cutting class. Pretty soon, Shakim dropped those habits. He and Dana became friends, often studying together.

"I knew from the start that he had the makings of a true friend," Latifah said. "He trusted me because I was honest with him from the beginning."

While she was making friends at Irvington, Dana still counted on her brother for advice and support. He never let her down. As a teenager, Winki dipped into his earnings from his after-school job to give Dana a weekly allowance. In exchange, she cleaned his room and ironed his clothes. "Winki was the one constant friend in my life," Latifah said. "Not only was he the man of the house after my parents split up, but he was also my protector and my soul mate."

RAP

Disc jockeys in the Bronx, New York, pioneered the techniques that became the foundation of rap. DJ (disc jockey) Kool Herc is often credited with inventing rap in the mid-1970s. A Jamaican immigrant, Herc brought the Jamaican tradition of "toasting" to Bronx nightclubs. When they toasted, Jamaican DJs spoke abbreviated words and sentences over music. A toast also boasted of the DJ's accomplishments and talents. Herc was also known for playing the "breaks"— parts of songs with the best beats. Those who danced during the breaks were called "break-dancers."

Another DJ, who called himself Grand Wizard, invented "scratching," the technique of moving the record player needle

across a record and using the scratching sound as a musical element. DJ Joseph "Grandmaster Flash" Sadler added "rappers" to his nightclub routine. While he mixed the music, his "emcees" or "MCs" (masters of ceremonies) rhymed to keep the audience dancing.

Rap artists drew on centuries-old African music and storytelling traditions, jive, modern African American street slang, and black pride and Black Power sentiments to express themselves. Rap quickly became very competitive as rappers competed for status and admiration from fans and fellow rappers.

The first rap song released by a record label hit stores in 1979. The SugarHill Gang's (below right) "Rapper's Delight" sold more than two million copies. This song introduced several key phrases of rap culture, including hip-hop, another word for rap.

Early rap was a male-dominated genre. Women were often portrayed negatively, and lyrics boasted of violence, sex, and abuse. One of the first female rappers, Roxanne Shanté, wrote her first rap in response to the group U.T.F.O.'s women-bashing rap, "Roxanne, Roxanne." Other female rappers emerged on the hip-hop scene to challenge their male counterparts. M.C. Lyte (facing page, top) and Sparky-D rapped about relationships, family and personal problems, and the difficult choices women face. Rappers Shazzy and Yo-Yo also tackled serious social issues in their raps.

At first, music critics did not quite know what to make of rap. Many refused to take the music seriously, dismissing rap as a fad. But rap's first superstars, including Run-D.M.C., LL Cool J (facing page, bottom), Public Enemy, and M.C. Hammer, proved that prediction wrong. Rap introduced an entire hip-hop culture and created a new vocabulary. Rap fans hung out in groups of friends they called "crews" and "posses." They used phrases such as "fresh" and "def" to praise. The words "bug," "wack," and "dis" expressed displeasure. A good friend was a "homeboy" or a "G." Neighborhoods were "the hood" and homes were "cribs." Rap fans were "b-boys" and "b-girls," the "b" short for break dancing. If they were "living large," they had become successful.

Winki and Dana were drawn to the country's newest musical sensation, rap. At Irvington High, rap caught on slowly, but Dana gravitated to those who shared her love of the new sound. There she met Ramsey Gdelawoe, who introduced her to hip-hop gear, which he bought in New York City boutiques.

Ramsey was an older high school student with his own apartment. Dana began hanging out there, enjoying the freedom to listen to and talk about rap for hours. Ramsey and his friends took Dana to rap clubs in New York City to experience live rap performances. Pretty soon, she was going clubbing as often as she could. Dana saw such acts as Grandmaster Flash, Dougie Fresh, and Run-D.M.C. She absorbed the sights and sounds of hip-hop culture.

"I was attracted to the sound and the content and the freedom of rap," Latifah said. "To me, it's like a free art form. It flows. It's smooth. It can be anything you want it to be."

Dana and Winki often decked themselves out in classic hip-hop gear—baggy pants and shirts, hooded sweatshirts, leather jackets, and unlaced sneakers. Dana took a job at Burger King to help pay for hip-hop albums and clothes. She practiced rapping as much as she could. During basketball season, her coach often suggested, "Dana, give us a little rap and cheer us up."

She even started her own group, called Ladies Fresh. She wrote her own lyrics, drawing on childhood memories and her African heritage. "Being Afrocentric and proud of my heritage, that's something I grew up with," Latifah said. "My mother always taught me that. When I started rapping, I wanted to make it part of my image."

Ladies Fresh's hip-hop performances lit up the Irvington stage and energized fans at basketball games. For a while, the trio was the only girl rap group at Irvington. Then another girl group challenged Ladies Fresh to a rap throw-down, daring the trio to prove their superiority. Latifah was energized by the competition.

"We stayed up all night writing stuff," Latifah remembered, "and I haven't stopped since."

Grandmaster Flash was a popular rapper at the Latin Quarter nightclub.

Dana began her professional singing career by rapping with the Flavor Unit in a friend's basement.

Chapter **FIVE**

THE FLAVOR UNIT

A COINCIDENTAL MEETING WITH AN INFLUENTIAL disc jockey propelled Dana even deeper into the world of rap. Mrs. Owens—who didn't even realize how obsessed her daughter was with rap—was actually the one who set Dana on her way. Mrs. Owens was responsible for selecting the entertainment for school events. She hired Mark The 45 King, a popular DJ who performed in clubs in the Bronx, to spin and mix records at an Irvington dance.

"I knew not to get a square DJ but one who really pumped it," Mrs. Owens said. "I heard Mark James play for another class and I just loved what he did."

Dana and Mark hit it off right away. Like Dana's friend Ramsey, Mark and his crew were a few years older than Dana. Almost every afternoon, Dana hung out at Mark's house, which was close to Irvington. His basement, filled with turntables and mixing equipment, drew young people who wanted to rap to Mark's mixing.

Once again, Dana found herself surrounded by male friends. Ramsey usually stopped by, and Shakim, Dana's study partner from geometry class, also became a regular fixture in Mark's basement. So did the performers known as Latee, Apache, Lakim, Chill Rob G, and Lord Alibaski. In time, this association of rappers called themselves the Flavor Unit. Used as a hip-hop term, *flavor* or *flava* means "special."

The rappers in the Flavor Unit became Dana's instructors and mentors. Ramsey emerged as the group's leader, encouraging everyone and motivating them with his vision and expectations. Because he believed so strongly in the Flavor Unit, Ramsey used his own money to further his friends' music careers. The first thing he had to do was to get their music in front of a disc jockey or record producer. Some of the Flavor Unit rappers recorded their raps on demo, or demonstration, tapes. Ramsey often used his rent money to pay for recording sessions in a nearby studio. Renting a recording studio is expensive. So the rappers practiced in Mark's basement until they were confident they could make a demo in just a few hours.

Recording a demonstration tape requires a recording studio, whether it is a professional place with state-of-the-art equipment or a small, low-budget operation. Thousands of hopeful stars make demos each year, recording their music on high-quality reel-to-reel tapes. Those with a lot of money can pay a recording studio to make hundreds of duplicate cassette tapes to send to record companies. Always on the lookout for new talent, record companies hire executives to listen to the onslaught of demo tapes they receive each year. Radio station disc jockeys also promote new talent, and if they like what they hear, they'll play a demo on the air.

"None of us [had] any money," Latifah remembered about the Flavor Unit. "We were broke kids but we had a lot of big dreams. Rap was how we wanted to make our money instead of being drug dealers."

At first, Dana was a little unsure of herself in Mark's basement. Hanging back, she listened to Mark's collection of rap albums and devoured issues of *Right On!* and *Word-Up,* the first hip-hop magazines.

"[I] studied rap inside and out," Latifah recalled. "It was like the training before the job."

Dana's self-confidence soon returned and she shed her shyness. Calling herself the Princess of the Posse because she was the only girl in the Flavor Unit, Dana started rapping for her friends. She let the beat of the music draw out her rhymes. This type of improvisation, called freestyling, is difficult. But Dana was up to the challenge.

"I knew I had it in me. I could hear in my head the

Some mainstream listeners discovered rap through groups such as Salt-N-Pepa.

way I wanted to sound," Latifah said. "It was just a matter of getting it from my brain to my voice."

After mixing songs in Mark's basement, the Flavor Unit rappers hit the streets to scope out the competition. They went to block parties and nightclubs in New Jersey and in the Bronx, Brooklyn, and Manhattan. Sometimes Dana stayed out all night, slipping back into her bedroom to catch a few hours of sleep before it was time to get up for school. She felt bad that she didn't tell her mother about her outings. But she knew that her mother worried about the violence in their community.

"Every weekend there was a major brawl," Latifah said about the club scene. "I'd watch somebody get robbed, then the bouncers would come in and tear the club up. It was like a ritual."

Dana and her friends often headed to the Latin Quarter, a hip-hop club in the somewhat seedy Times

Square district. In the mid-1980s, the Latin Quarter was very popular among teens, who were allowed to attend the club but were not served alcohol. The club—with its black walls, many dance floors, and strobe lights—drew the hottest rappers of the day. Dana and her posse danced to the live music of rappers Run-D.M.C. and Kool Moe Dee. Female rapper MC Lyte and rap music's first major female group, Salt-N-Pepa, also appeared at the Latin Quarter.

"When I came onto the scene, rap was entering a new phase," Latifah said. "It was not just simple rhymes over the most popular songs; the music was about saying something. . . . And simply by being there, I was one of the people making the culture. It was amazing to be a part of such a force."

Run-D.M.C. drew huge crowds at New York City clubs in the mid-1980s.

Rap was no longer a single type of music. New styles emerged. They included the hard-core "gangsta" rap, the lighter pop rap, and an Afrocentric rap with lyrics that embraced African nationalism. One night, during a hip-hop performance at the Latin Quarter, Dana for the first time seriously considered a future as a rapper. In 1986, there were few female rappers. Those like Salt-N-Pepa, who did break into the male-dominated hip-hop scene, looked and acted nothing like Dana. Still athletic, Dana wore comfortable clothes and kept her hair cropped short or pulled into a pony-tail. She had little in common with female rappers who wore skimpy outfits and looked like models.

Then along came female rapper duo Sweet Tee and DJ Jazzy Joyce. They tore up the stage at the Latin Quarter with their masterful mixes and dressed-down but confident stage presence.

"I saw someone who looked like me doing some-thing I'd only imagined doing," Latifah said. "Sweet Tee and Jazzy Joyce were just regular girls in their Adidas sweat suits. Until them, it had never really oc-curred to me that I could be up there, rocking the house."

In the meantime, Dana was enjoying a busy senior year. She continued to heat things up on the basket-ball court. A five-foot-ten-inch powerhouse of speed and precision, Dana led her team to another state championship, scoring the winning point with just one second left in the game. At the end of the school year, the class of 1987 voted Dana "Best All Around," "Most Popular," "Most Comical," and "Best Dancer" in Irvington's senior class poll.

After graduating from high school, Dana decided to study broadcast journalism at the Borough of Manhattan Community College. She began classes that summer. But with thoughts of a music career in the back of her mind, she considered all her options. Perhaps she could do something with her raps. She might even get a song on the radio. She had to try.

With financial help from her friend Ramsey, Dana went to a small studio the summer after graduation to record a demo tape. She rapped two songs, "Princess of the Posse" and "Wrath of My Madness." In just a few hours, she had a tape in hand.

"From the start, my style was different," Latifah said. "I sang the intro and rapped in a Jamaican dialect. Nobody was doing that back then."

When the recording session was over, Dana and Ramsey exchanged knowing smiles. "We knew it was good," Latifah said of her first recording.

They were right. One afternoon a few weeks later, Dana was listening to music in the kitchen of the Owenses' East Orange apartment. As she turned the radio dial trying to tune in a good station, she heard the opening lines of "Princess of the Posse."

"My record. My song. Me. Playing on the radio. I was so excited I just ran to the window and screamed out 'My record is on the radio! My record is on the radio!' " Latifah wrote in her autobiography. And the news was about to get even better.

Mark The 45 King had given Dana's demo to Fred "Fab 5 Freddy" Braithwaite, host of *Yo! MTV Raps,* a new program on the Music Television network (MTV). Freddy liked what he heard and knew that this unknown teen from East Orange, New Jersey, was special. Not only were her lyrics and sound different, but she was different from any other rapper he had heard. "She had a dignity and a kind of regal quality and street sense [but] was feminine and womanly at the same time," Freddy remembered.

Freddy gave Dana's demo to Tommy Boy Records, a label known for signing rap artists. Latifah caught the

Fab 5 Freddy helped jump-start Dana's singing career. Freddy, the host of Yo! MTV Raps, *passed along Dana's demo tape to Tommy Boy Records, which signed her right away.*

attention of Tommy Boy executive Monica Lynch. A few days after hearing her song on the radio, Dana—hot and sweaty from playing basketball—picked up the phone to hear Monica Lynch on the line wanting to talk about a record contract.

"It was frightening because it happened so quickly," Dana's mom remembered. "Tommy Boy was calling the house and two days later we signed on the dotted line."

But Dana handled the opportunity with her typical finesse. She met with executives at Tommy Boy Records to discuss the terms of the contract.

"She impressed everyone," Monica Lynch remembered. "You could tell she was something special."

While it looked like her dedication was about to pay off, Dana remained cautious. She knew how difficult it was to become successful as a rapper, especially for women. Female rappers such as Roxanne Shanté, Monie Love, M.C. Lyte, and Salt-N-Pepa had broken into the industry, but their success was no guarantee for Dana. Not about to gamble her whole future, Dana decided that for the time being, she would pursue a music career *and* stay in college.

"Becoming a rapper didn't just happen overnight," Latifah said. "Subconsciously I had been preparing for it most of my life. The music lessons. The talent shows. All those nights at the clubs, the endless hours in DJ Mark The 45 King's basement, the practicing, the reading, prepared me for something. . . . But I was raised to always have something to fall back on."

Dana became Queen Latifah complete with a "crown"—to show her pride in her African heritage.

Chapter **SIX**

THE QUEEN HAS ARRIVED

ALTHOUGH **DANA HAD RECORDED HER DEMO** singles under the name Latifah, she wanted a stage name with greater grab. She considered calling herself MC Latifah. But she knew that to distinguish herself from other rappers, she would need a unique name—a name that represented her values and beliefs.

She thought back through her life for inspiration. She remembered the passionate conversations with friends and family about apartheid in South Africa and racial injustices in the United States. She relived the times when her parents proudly told her that she was descended from the kings and queens who once ruled the African continent. She thought about how her mother had taught her to live with dignity, to hold her head high, to always believe in herself. She remembered the other strong women in her life—her grandmothers and aunts. Dana realized that she could honor all these women with the name she selected.

So Dana Owens became Queen Latifah. She chose the name, she said, "not to denote rank, but to acknowledge that all black people come from a long line of kings and queens that they've never known about. This is my way of giving tribute to them."

Latifah also wanted to honor her mother, who provided her with a strong foundation and room to stretch her wings. "In many ways, she was the queen who gave me the guts and the confidence to become one myself," Latifah said. "She gave birth, physically and spiritually, to Queen Latifah."

Gangsta rappers, including the group N.W.A., above, **wrote lyrics that degraded women and glorified violence and promiscuous sex.**

As a rapper, Latifah wanted to offer an alternative to the graphic and profane lyrics of male artists who portrayed women as sexual objects. Gangsta rappers such as Ice T, Ice Cube, N.W.A., Dr. Dre, and Snoop Doggy Dogg often sang about violence, promiscuous sex, and the brutalization of women. Lyrics also glamorized gang activity and drug use.

Latifah herself sometimes used profanity in her lyrics. But she said that her intentions were different than those of gangsta rappers. "It's the way the word is used," Latifah explained. "When it's used to downgrade or denigrate you, that's when I have a problem with it being used toward women."

Many people blamed songs like Ice T's "Cop Killer" and 2 Live Crew's album *As Nasty As They Wanna Be* for the increasing violence in U.S. cities. Although the First Amendment of the U.S. Constitution grants Americans the right of free speech, many citizens called for regulations to control rap lyrics.

While Latifah denounced the sexism and violence in some groups' lyrics, she agreed with their social and political messages. She also supported the rappers' constitutional right to express opinions in their lyrics. "A lot of what these guys are saying needs to be heard," she said. "They're bringing reality—the reality of the black culture—to a lot of people, pointing out things and exposing things that might be ignored otherwise."

Latifah felt that her own message was equally important and needed to be heard, especially by young black women. Her songs encouraged women to be independent and act with dignity, just as she had been taught to do. Her rapping was a way to share the lessons she had learned from her mother.

Tommy Boy gave Latifah money to outfit herself for promotional pictures. She used the opportunity to cement her image as a strong, self-respecting black woman. She went to an African clothing store in Newark and asked the owner to design a regal-looking outfit. She also purchased accessories, including a crownlike hat. Unable to find shoes she liked, she posed barefoot for her first publicity photographs. "People noticed me because I wasn't looking like everybody else," she said.

In 1988 Tommy Boy Records released "Wrath Of My Madness" as a single. Latifah and Monica Lynch were encouraged when it sold forty-thousand copies. Latifah worked steadily over the next year and released two more singles, "Dance With Me" and, with British rapper Monie Love, "Ladies First."

"Ladies First" is a testimony to the many black women who worked for the liberation of their people in the United States, South Africa, and elsewhere in the world where blacks received unequal treatment. The powerful single became Latifah's first hit on the rhythm and blues charts. The song eventually was included in the Rock and Roll Hall of Fame's "500 Songs That Shaped Rock and Roll."

As her music career demanded more and more of

Queen Latifah performs to support AIDS research and other social causes. Here she takes the stage at a danceathon for AIDS in New York City.

her time, Latifah made the difficult decision to leave school. She promised herself that one day she would return to complete her degree. She also made another major life change when she moved out of the apartment she shared with her mother and brother and found her own place.

In 1989, Latifah released her first album, *All Hail The Queen,* to critical acclaim. One critic warned other rappers, "Male rappers step off, because the queen has arrived." Another described Latifah as "singing from the heart with the influence of the mind." Her debut album eventually sold one million copies and climbed to number six on the *Billboard* rhythm and blues chart.

All Hail The Queen was different from other rap albums. Latifah, like other rappers, used her music to

With her regal crowns, colorful outfits, and strong messages, Queen Latifah quickly distinguished herself from other rappers.

voice opinions on a variety of social issues and to promote black pride. But unlike most other rappers, Latifah wrote from a woman's point of view. In songs like "Latifah's Law" and "Mama Gave Birth to the Soul Children," she explored the lives of young black women.

Latifah's music appealed to a broad audience, including pop and alternative rock fans, because she rapped to a variety of background sounds, including reggae and jazz. In yet another departure from tradition, Latifah became one of the few rappers to both rap and sing on her album.

By the time Latifah's first album hit record stores, the Afrocentrism that characterized her music had become a popular cultural movement across the United States. The phrase *Afrocentric* was first used in 1976 by Molefi Kete Asante, a professor at Temple University in Philadelphia. He supported the study of African history and culture from a non-European perspective. Many black Americans adopted African ways and studied African history. Around the time *All Hail The Queen* came out, other rappers, including X-clan, the Jungle Brothers, and Public Enemy, incorporated Afrocentric themes into their music and stage presence. They began wearing clothes made from kente cloth, a traditional African material.

"Afrocentricity is about being into yourself and into your people and being proud of your origins," Latifah said. "I was lucky to grow up in a very cultured family, and so Afrocentricity is something I've known all my life."

To promote her debut album, Latifah embarked on a European tour and continued performing in the United States. Onstage, she made sure her fans not only heard but also *saw* her message of dignity and self-respect. She refused to wear skimpy or revealing outfits. She expected the same from those who performed alongside her.

"Sex sells, that's common sense," she said. "A lot of women sell their bodies. . . . That's not what I feel I need to do to sell a record. I'm not willing to sacrifice who I am."

Latifah also knew that her music had another important mission—to create racial tolerance and unity. Critics were already praising the Queen for expanding the boundaries of rap. Her unique style appealed to fans of different races, breaking barriers and busting stereotypes.

Latifah enjoyed touring and performing, but she quickly realized that she lacked the skills to handle the business side of her music career. Without a road manager to collect payments after her shows, she found herself vulnerable to promoters who sometimes shortchanged her.

Historically, black performers have been exploited by the white-controlled music industry. In the early days of rock and roll, some white record producers cheated talented black songwriters and performers, using their material without paying them. Misleading contracts and falsified financial statements were used to steal money and recognition from black performers.

After one of Latifah's concerts in Connecticut, a stubborn promoter wouldn't pay her the fee they had agreed upon in earlier negotiations. Latifah's old high school friend Shakim was at the concert that night. He volunteered to collect the payment.

"I don't know what he said to this promoter, but he returned in ten minutes with every penny I was owed," Latifah remembered. "Shakim knew how to take care of business. I had watched him grow from the lanky boy in my geometry class to a man who seized responsibility."

Latifah saw that she needed someone to nurture her career. She turned to the people she trusted the most.

Shakim quit his job and became Latifah's road manager. Mrs. Owens, still teaching art at Irvington High School, took on an expanded role in her daughter's career.

By the time Latifah went on tour to Europe, she had expanded her wardrobe of African-style outfits. She rarely performed without a "crown." The regal look had become her trademark.

Latifah's popularity grew when her first music videos were broadcast to MTV's international audiences. In the "Ladies First" video, Latifah and Monie Love rap alongside film clips of black protests and giant photographs of influential black women, such as abolitionist Sojourner Truth and activist Angela Davis. To spread her anti-apartheid message, Latifah dressed in a military uniform and walked across a map of South Africa. The power of white men was symbolically replaced with sculptures of fists raised in the Black Power salute.

"I wanted to show the strength of black women in history," Latifah said. "I wanted to show what we've done. Sisters have been in the midst of things for a long time."

Monie Love, who was the same age as Latifah, shared Latifah's positive image. Like the Queen, she tackled serious themes in her songs. "It's refreshing to see when girls like myself and Latifah come out with positive stuff," Monie Love said. "Ladies are doing things just as much as men are, and actions speak louder than words."

Queen Latifah, shown here in a powerful stance, hoped for strength and unity within black communities. She expressed her strong opinions through her music—and her appearance.

By collaborating with her "competitors," Latifah stood apart from an important characteristic of the rap industry—the competition between rappers. Male rap artists especially were known for the infighting in their song lyrics. Women rappers sometimes employed boastful one-upmanship. But Latifah rarely glorified herself in her raps. When she did, her approach was witty instead of insulting.

"There's room for everybody," Latifah once said. "I don't feel threatened when other girls put out good records—I feel motivated to make a good record as well."

As Latifah became better known, movie producers approached her with acting opportunities. Although her career was still young, Latifah's intelligence, thoughtful lyrics, and sense of social responsibility had already wowed executives throughout the entertainment industry. Latifah jumped at the chance to make movies. She accepted a role in Spike Lee's urban drama *Jungle Fever*.

"I love acting because I get to do things I might not do in real life," Latifah said. "It's fun, but a lot of hard work. When you see the finished deal, though, you know it was worth the energy and effort."

When *Jungle Fever* was released in 1991, Latifah impressed audiences and reviewers. She plays a waitress who is angered when a black customer brings his white girlfriend to a restaurant in Harlem, a black neighborhood in New York City. The poised, confident Latifah delivered her lines with a feisty, no-nonsense attitude. Her on-screen appearance was brief. But it was clear that Latifah had the potential to be as good an actor as she was a rapper. One critic called her a "royal talent."

Queen Latifah with her mother, Rita Owens

Chapter **SEVEN**

LIVING LARGE

THE 1990s WELCOMED QUEEN LATIFAH WITH awards, praise, and new opportunities. In 1990 the readers of *Rolling Stone* magazine voted her Best Female Rapper. The largest music industry convention in the nation, the New Music Seminar in New York City, named her Best New Artist of 1990. Critics continued to praise her upbeat songs and to recognize her potential beyond the world of rap.

Latifah's messages even found their way into the classrooms of the nation's universities. Within a year of the release of *All Hail The Queen,* students at Harvard University were studying Latifah's music. They were discussing the cultural impact of her lyrics and her commitment to creating positive images in rap.

Latifah felt honored when Harvard invited her to speak at the university.

"It's a great feeling to know that people listen to you, that what you say makes a difference to them," Latifah said.

Some of the biggest stars in the music industry were also paying attention to the rising Queen. When rock superstar David Bowie remade his 1970s hit song "Fame," he invited Latifah to collaborate. Male rappers asked her to appear in their videos, hoping her presence would win over female fans. Many music critics credited Queen Latifah, whose thoughtful lyrics supported racial and gender harmony, with raising the respectability of rap music.

Already a strong presence in the music world and an emerging movie star, the Queen turned next to television. In 1990, executives at the ABC network invited Latifah to make her television debut on an Earth Day special. The two-hour program celebrated the twentieth anniversary of the environmental holiday Earth Day. The show featured some of the biggest names in the entertainment industry, including Barbra Streisand, Robin Williams, the cast of *The Cosby Show*, and basketball star Magic Johnson.

Soon Latifah was making regular television appearances on talk shows, variety shows, and sitcoms, including *In Living Color, Roc,* and *Hangin' with Mr. Cooper.* She regularly appeared in "Rock the Vote" and other public service announcements.

D. J. Jazzy Jeff (Jeffrey Townes), left, *and The Fresh Prince (Will Smith),* right, *rapped together in the late 1980s. Smith's TV sitcom,* The Fresh Prince of Bel-Air, *took off in the 1990s and helped rap become better known in mainstream society.*

In 1990, the multitalented, Emmy award-winning rapper Will Smith asked Latifah to make guest appearances on his popular television program, *The Fresh Prince of Bel-Air. The Fresh Prince* became one of the most successful African American–centered television programs of all time. Many reviewers credit Will Smith with smoothing the way for other rappers—including Latifah—to make the jump into prime-time series television.

Determined to pursue an acting career, Latifah quickly accepted roles in *House Party 2* and *Juice,* movies about urban African American youth. As Latifah's career took off, she watched her friends from the Flavor Unit struggle to find outlets for their music. They too had run into crooked club managers like the one who tried to cheat the Queen during her first concert tour. "Many of us were so uneducated in business matters that we're constantly getting duped while filling the pockets of record companies," she said.

Anxious to help these talented artists, Latifah transformed her circle of friends into a formal business. Called Flavor Unit Management, the business is headquartered in Jersey City, New Jersey. "Flavor Unit began as a support system to just help sort out all the business dealings," she said.

Although she was the chief executive officer, Latifah relied on her mother and friends to oversee the company's day-to-day operations. Flavor Unit Management began by managing the careers of the rap trio Naughty By Nature. As Naughty By Nature took off, other groups flocked to Flavor Unit. The company quickly grew into a successful management business, representing scores of artists, including Apache, LL Cool J, Outkast, N.E.X.T, and Monica.

Owning an entertainment management business also gave Latifah a base from which to oversee her own growing career. Latifah felt she was losing the artistic freedom that was so important to her. She found herself at odds with executives at Tommy Boy. Flavor Unit offered her an alternative. "I wanted to control my own destiny," Latifah said.

A growing movie career did not keep Latifah from her music. Working hard to please her fans, she released *Nature Of A Sista* in late 1991. Like *All Hail The Queen,* Latifah's second album continued to break down barriers between rap and mainstream music. "I've become more creative with melodies and things like that," she said. "I am singing more and this album is really rhythmic."

But her raps remained true Queen Latifah. She tackled such issues as violence and teen pregnancy and continued to promote the benefits of self-respect, hard work, and black pride. In her song "Nuff of the Ruff Stuff," Latifah praised the power of self-confidence and a positive attitude.

The rap trio Naughty By Nature, with Queen Latifah, center, *was the first band managed by Queen Latifah's company, Flavor Unit Management.*

In "One Mo' Time," she asked young black women to take responsibility for their lives, telling them that they must respect themselves before others will respect them. In "Fly Girl," which was nominated for a Grammy Award, she reminded men to respect women. "Bad As A Mutha" scolded girls and women for being materialistic and status conscious, dating men only for their money or fancy cars. "There are a lot of girls out there who do that, and that's what I'm trying to change," Latifah explained.

She promoted her second album by joining reggae artist Ziggy Marley on a national tour, performing nearly three hundred shows in one year. By this time, Latifah had abandoned her regal attire, afraid that fans were more interested in the royal theme than in what she was trying to say in her music.

"I stopped wearing the crowns because people seemed to get too caught up in that," she said. "I'm more than just a hat."

As soon as she was financially able, Latifah began to practice what she preached by investing in her community. She gave back to her East Orange community by purchasing businesses and providing jobs for inner-city residents. One of her ventures was Videos To Go, a movie rental store that delivered.

At age twenty-one, Latifah was experiencing the success that she and the other Flavor Unit rappers had fantasized about in DJ Mark The 45 King's basement. Her life was a dizzying whirl of recording sessions, concert dates, promotional events, movie sets, fan letters, and public appearances. Reporters, fans, music critics, journalists, and politicians were talking about her in ways that she had never even imagined. In October 1991, *Sassy*, a magazine for teenage girls, even nominated her for president!

Latifah's success did not surprise her mother. "I've always taught her to set goals, accomplish them, and set higher goals," she said. "She took me very seriously, and it's nice to know that some of the things you teach your children really do stick."

Latifah's impressive rise to stardom did not protect her from problems experienced every day by black Americans, however. While much of the world looked at Queen Latifah and saw a successful entertainer and role model, police officers often viewed her suspiciously. Latifah described being stopped by police officers who wanted to know why a young black woman was driving such a fancy car—an expensive BMW.

"What do you mean what am I doing with this car?" she would respond. "I earned this car. I paid for it in cash, in full."

"I can't tell you how many times I've been stopped," she told a reporter in late 1991. Incidents like these were a source of frustration and sadness for Latifah, especially since they reflected the social problems she criticized in her musical mix.

Queen Latifah loved to spend time with her brother, Winki. They often rode motorcycles together.

Chapter **EIGHT**

WINKI

LIKE HIS FAMOUS SISTER, WINKI OWENS HAD FOUND his own version of success. After high school, he remained in New Jersey to be close to his family. Following in his father's footsteps, he trained at the police academy and joined the Newark police force.

Although Dana and Winki had independent lives, the bond between them remained strong. This connection made it difficult for them to be apart, without the regular interaction they were used to. With the hard work of writing, recording, performing, and touring, Latifah's schedule was so busy that she sometimes didn't see her mother and brother for weeks.

When Winki and Latifah did find time to be together, the two liked to hop on their motorcycles and ride for miles. Winki had fallen in love with the power of two-wheelers before his sister, but she soon became a devoted rider. For his twenty-fourth birthday, she and her mother gave Winki his second motorcycle, a powerful Kawasaki Ninja.

"When we were on the road together, we had a free, wild feeling that nothing else gave us," Latifah said. "When we took our bikes on the open road, it was our private realm. Out there, no one could bother us. We were one."

The little time Latifah did spend with Winki and her mother reminded her how much she needed her family. And she wanted to repay her mother and brother for all they had done for her.

She began hunting for a home to share with her mother and brother. She envisioned a house that would give them each a personal space, but still allow for the family togetherness they all wanted and needed. In nearby Wayne, New Jersey, she found a large, unfinished house that she could custom-design.

Despite her celebrity and huge financial success, Latifah faced discrimination when she applied for a mortgage. She found out that not much had changed in the years since her mother had been denied a home loan. "Queen Latifah could not get a mortgage," the star said incredulously. "I had to go through three different companies. If I had to go through this, I can imagine what everybody else has to go through."

Once she had secured a mortgage, Latifah began to

make sketches of the house. But as she planned her own dream home, she also promised herself that some-day she would help develop affordable housing for low-income residents in her community. She wanted to ensure that buyers were treated with respect.

As she watched the house take shape, Latifah imag-ined all the good times she would share with Winki and her mother in the years to come. But a few weeks before the house was finished, a tragic accident de-stroyed Latifah's plan to reunite her family.

In April 1992, twenty-four-year-old Winki was riding his birthday motorcycle around East Orange, New Jer-sey. A collision with a car sent his bike spinning out of control.

Latifah and Shakim were helping a friend move when Ramsey telephoned with the news. Too shaken to drive, Latifah asked Shakim to take her to the hos-pital. As they drove, a chill spread through her body. Ramsey had not told her how serious the accident was, or that Winki was near death. But Latifah knew.

Just three days earlier, Dana and Winki had taken their bikes out for a spin. Afterward, they hugged and for the last time she told her brother she loved him.

Following Winki's death, Latifah entered the lowest point of her life. "I loved him so much that I didn't want to live," she remembered. "If I couldn't share my life, my successes, my dreams, and my thoughts with him, it wasn't worth it."

Consumed by grief and anger, she lost control. Her

strength and discipline weren't enough to cope with the pain of losing her brother. To make matters worse, she blamed herself for his death. "I never imagined that bike, bought out of love, would be the cause of Winki's death," she said.

In the weeks and months after the funeral, Latifah looked for ways to numb her pain. She spent hours on the basketball court, taking out her anger with every shot. She used alcohol and drugs to shut out her feelings. She walked around in a daze and wore sunglasses to hide her tears.

After Winki's death, Latifah had difficulty concentrating on her work. "When Winki died, the song in me died," she said. But she knew her brother would have wanted her to fulfill her obligations. As her strength and focus slowly returned, she forced herself back into the studio to work on her third album, *Black Reign*, which she was making with her new label, Motown Records.

In the song "Winki's Theme," she paid tribute to her big brother. He had watched over her when he was alive and, she believed, continued to do so after his death.

But it would take a long time to heal. It seemed like Latifah could not do anything without being reminded of her loss. When she visited her Grandmother Bray, she was drawn to the room where family photographs were proudly displayed. "I can still see the hurt in her," her grandmother, Katherine Bray, remarked.

After the accident, Latifah could not bring herself to ride her motorcycle. For the first time in her life, fear overcame her. The motorcycle reminded her that she was powerless to control the forces of life and death. When she thought about riding the bike, she was afraid that she might die too, leaving her mother childless.

After finding strength in her music and renewing her relationship with God, Latifah, in time, shed her fear and guilt. The day came when she could finally look at her motorcycle without hating it. She wheeled it onto the road, started the engine, and took off. As she sped along the highway, she allowed herself to re-member the happy times she and Winki had spent to-gether on the open road. As she guided the motorcycle, Latifah touched her hand to her heart to feel the chain around her neck. As a memorial to her brother's life, she had put the key to Winki's motor-cycle on a necklace and pledged to always wear it.

Coming to grips with her brother's death was the hardest challenge the young star had faced in her life. But she knew she had to move forward to meet what-ever awaited her.

"The road back is the road to healing yourself," she said. "When you find it, it's like a light that shines just on you. Then you just start taking this walk and you don't know what's coming, but you're not afraid of it."

Queen Latifah, front, *with her costars in the TV sitcom* Living Single

Chapter **NINE**

LIVING SINGLE

WHILE THE TIME FOLLOWING WINKI'S DEATH WAS very difficult for Latifah, her professional achievements and her popularity continued to soar. She released her third album, *Black Reign*, in late 1993, and she dedicated it to Winki. For the CD cover, she chose a photograph of herself sitting next to her brother's grave. "'I Love U & Miss U more than words could ever express," she wrote on the cover.

On *Black Reign*, in addition to rapping, Latifah did more traditional singing than on her first two albums. The range of her songs, from rap to rhythm and blues to jazz, established her as singer of immense talent. *Black Reign* was a hot seller and became the first gold record by a solo female rap artist.

After the release of *Black Reign,* Latifah shifted her creative energies to focus on her acting career. Her first major dramatic role was in the 1993 movie *My Life.* The movie stars Michael Keaton as Bob Jones, a man who makes a video autobiography when he is diagnosed with terminal cancer. Critics praised Latifah for her performance as Theresa, the nurse who cares for Jones toward the end of his life. She helps him and his family accept his death.

Fox television network was impressed by Latifah's versatility as an actor. Executives offered her a lead role in a new situation comedy about young black professional women pursuing careers in New York City. Fox producer Yvette Lee Bowser created the show, which was called *Living Single.* She hoped to provide African American viewers with intelligent and successful female role models.

Accepting a role on *Living Single* meant leaving New Jersey to live in Los Angeles during the production season. But Latifah was drawn to the sitcom. Like her music, it cast black women in a positive light rather than in negative stereotypes. Latifah wrote the show's theme song, and the first episode aired in August 1993.

Living Single revolved around the lives of roommates Khadijah (Latifah), her cousin Synclaire (Kim Coles), and their friends Regine (Kim Fields) and Maxine (Erika Alexander). The role of magazine publisher Khadijah James was a natural choice for Latifah. A strong and determined entrepreneur, Khadijah founded *Flavor*, a magazine for women. She worked hard to make it succeed. Like Latifah, Khadijah surrounded herself with family and longtime friends. With sharp intelligence and a quick wit, Khadijah was often cast in the role of mediator and negotiator. She was the group's anchor. Khadijah was an outstanding role model for the black community.

But Latifah sometimes had trouble enjoying being the star of a popular television show. "I'm on TV but it doesn't mean what it should because I'm not feeling all the way," she said. "I wish my brother were here just to experience some of this with me."

The characters of Living Single—*played by,* left to right, *Queen Latifah, Kim Fields, Erika Alexander, and Kim Coles—were role models for African American women.*

Latifah lived thousands of miles from the Flavor Unit Management company. But she kept tabs on her business, which had grown to ten full-time employees by 1994. During filming breaks, she listened to demo tapes and reviewed the financial and business reports her staff express-mailed to her each week.

Filming a weekly television show is exhausting work that requires a strict schedule. Actors report to the studio as early as 6 A.M. and may work fourteen to sixteen hours a day. Like other shows, *Living Single* took a break each summer. During these months, Latifah was free to pursue movie roles and spend time writing and recording. But during the normal production schedule, from late summer through spring, time was tight. Latifah settled into a demanding routine.

Between taping the show and running Flavor Unit, Latifah still somehow found time to pursue new interests. She learned kickboxing. No matter how tired she was, she enjoyed checking out the Los Angeles nightclub scene. As she left a club one evening, not long after arriving in Los Angeles, Latifah met Ferric Collons, a football player with the Los Angeles Raiders.

As a star, Latifah often felt that her success intimidated men and kept her from having genuine relationships. But Latifah didn't feel this way when she was with Ferric. They both had successful careers. Instead of worrying about her boyfriend's ego and making sure he was having a good time, Latifah could relax and enjoy herself. The two had a lot in common, particularly sports. Latifah enjoyed Ferric's attentiveness to *her* needs.

In August 1995, the Los Angeles Raiders traded Ferric to the New England Patriots. With three thousand miles separating them and careers demanding their attention, Latifah and Ferric could not hold onto their romantic relationship. They remained good friends, however.

Meanwhile, *Living Single* had become an instant hit among viewers. At the end of its first season, it was the Fox network's best-rated new program. Soon it was the most-watched show in African American households. And in 1995, the National Association for the Advancement of Colored People (NAACP) named *Living Single* the best comedy at its annual Image Awards.

The year got even better. At the Soul Train Music Awards, Latifah was presented with the Sammy Davis, Jr. Award for Entertainer of the Year. And on March 1, 1995, Latifah joined hundreds of music stars in Los Angeles for the thirty-seventh annual Grammy Awards. In addition to being nominated for her second Grammy, Queen Latifah was asked to present an award. That night, she won what many believed was a long-overdue Grammy Award. Her song "U.N.I.T.Y." was chosen as the best rap solo performance of 1994. More than one billion viewers in sixteen countries watched as she accepted the award.

Latifah wrote the song "U.N.I.T.Y." after witnessing

abusive behavior between men and women at a picnic in Philadelphia. The song is a salute to women. It also reminds listeners that disrespect, insults, and physical abuse work against unity among black people.

The joy of winning a Grammy was soon overshadowed by the violence she criticized in her music. In July 1995, while Latifah was driving with friends in Harlem, two black youths carjacked her BMW. They shot her bodyguard and close friend, Shawn Moon, almost killing him.

"I ran to him so quickly that I left my sandals behind," Latifah remembered. Without stopping to think, she stepped into traffic and flagged down passing cars until a driver stopped and drove Shawn to the hospital.

A police detective who investigated the carjacking praised Latifah's quick thinking. "It was probably what saved [Moon's] life," he said. "Here she was, a victim of a crime in a stressful situation, and she was calm, cool, and collected."

The carjackers were quickly caught and later tried and jailed. But the incident changed Latifah, and she would never be the same. She hired more bodyguards, and for a while she rarely went out to nightclubs or parties.

In time, Latifah wrote about the carjacking in a song she called "Must Have Been An Angel." She dealt with her fear by carrying a gun. A few months after the attack, she was stopped for speeding in Los Angeles.

When police searched her car, they found a loaded pistol and marijuana. They arrested her.

As a result of her arrest, Latifah was fined, given two years' probation, and required to make a donation to a Los Angeles charity. The negative news about a positive rap star was difficult for Latifah. She has often said it isn't easy being a role model. "Some people put you on a pedestal and don't let you be human. You're forced to feeling you should be perfect. That's not a comfortable thing."

Fully aware that she set an example for thousands of young people, Latifah was disturbed that her fans would learn about her drug use. She worked hard to let kids know that she had made a mistake and had used poor judgment.

But Latifah did not let the painful incidents of 1995 weaken her determination. "When the bad things happen, she never lets that discourage her," said Shakim. "She kept following the game plan. That comes from her mother."

Meanwhile, Latifah's portrayal of the down-to-earth Khadijah introduced even more fans to her work. Movie producers continued to approach her with acting roles. Latifah found herself choosing from many offers, and she made her decisions carefully.

"First, I read the script and decide if I like my place in the film," she said. "I read the role to see if it is meaty, to see if it is something I can get into, something I feel I am capable of doing, something challenging. Then I look at who is involved with it, directing it, and starring in it. I look at the whole package, the chemistry, and the track record of whoever is involved."

Latifah surprised fans by accepting a role in the violent film *Set It Off,* which was released in 1996 and featured her own single "Name Calling." In the movie, four young black women resort to robbing banks as a means of escaping their dead-end lives in a Los Angeles ghetto. Friends since childhood, the four characters are united by their common plight—low-paying jobs, sexism, and racism. One character loses her younger brother when police kill him in a case of mistaken identity. Another character must give up her toddler son when a social worker decides she is an unfit mother.

Despite her opposition to violence, Latifah accepted the role of Cleo, a tough young woman working as a janitor. She believed the film conveyed important messages about the lives of black Americans. More social drama than action film, *Set It Off* portrayed the hopelessness and violence that Latifah witnessed growing up in Hyatt Court and later in East Orange.

She was also drawn to the role of Cleo, a lesbian who drinks too much and takes drugs, because she wanted an acting challenge. "Cleo was so not me that I had to work hard on becoming that person and proving that I could do it, that I could act," Latifah said.

Latifah's performance received high praise from film

critics, including the well-known Roger Ebert. He gave the movie three and a half stars out of a possible four. Another reviewer applauded Latifah's versatility and her willingness to play a somewhat negative character. Another critic proclaimed, "[Latifah] is the best thing about the movie: She dominates every scene she's in."

In 1997 Latifah took the Best Actress award at the Black Film Awards. At the Independent Film Awards that year, she won an award for best supporting actress.

Unfortunately, *Set It Off* spurred gang and other violence in southern California, Washington, D.C., and New York City. Latifah was saddened by the news of the film's effect. She was discouraged that viewers were getting the wrong message about using violence to solve problems. "The women [in the film] definitely make the wrong choice. Definitely," she said. "They lose everything."

As Latifah's acting career flourished, so did her management company. Flavor Unit Management was representing ten groups. With the launch of her own record label in 1995, Latifah moved from managing artists to recording them. In 1996 Flavor Unit Entertainment opened a West Coast management office to represent rhythm and blues artist Monica and other singers based in California. Latifah asked her old friend Ramsey Gdelawoe to head the California operation as general manager.

"It's incredible to look back over the years and see how far we've come," said the twenty-eight-year-old

Queen Latifah promoted the film Set It Off *in 1996.*

Latifah. "I've always believed that someone who's moving up should always take the time to look back and give a hand to the next young person trying to make some moves."

Potential clients appreciated Latifah's philosophy. "[Flavor Unit has] accomplished something," said rapper Daddy D, who recorded his first single on the Flavor Unit label. "They're growing and that's the team I want to be on."

As one part of Latifah's career was expanding,

another was winding down. Although *Living Single* continued to be a hit with viewers, executives at Fox surprised the cast when they canceled the show at the end of the 1996–97 season. Shocked by the news, thousands of fans across the country wrote letters protesting the cancellation. The network brought back the show for another season.

"I'd like to thank everyone who put in the effort to tell Fox how they felt," Latifah told a reporter in 1997. "You have to pay a certain amount of respect to the people who are making you a lot of money and bringing a lot of attention to your network. Fox needed to think about that."

Teenage girls in 1997 ranked Latifah among the top ten television personalities they enjoyed. All the same, *Living Single* was canceled after five seasons, and the show went into syndication—shown in repeats. Cancellation did not minimize the program's effect. One year after it ended, *Living Single* received a second NAACP Image Award for best television comedy.

"I was sad that I was losing the daily camaraderie of my friends; hanging out everyday and doing something fun, making people laugh and giving the fans a show they enjoyed," Latifah said soon after the show was canceled. "But I'm also excited about the future and being free to do more things in terms of films. There's always going to be life after *Living Single*."

Queen Latifah's father, Lancelot Owens, right, *escorted Latifah to the 1997 Soul Train Lady of Soul Awards.*

Chapter **TEN**

LONG LIVE
THE QUEEN

LIFE AFTER *LIVING SINGLE* WAS AS FAST-PACED AS Latifah had hoped it would be. In 1997 she won the Aretha Franklin Award for Entertainer of the Year at the Soul Train Lady of Soul Awards. She was profiled on Lifetime Television's *Intimate Portrait* series. And she played an enthusiastic gambler in the action movie *Hoodlum,* a look into the 1930s world of organized crime in Harlem. The Queen's status as a veteran rapper was acknowledged when she was invited to participate in *Fat Beats & Bra Straps.* This CD collection celebrates the rise of women in hip-hop.

The following year, Latifah tackled a variety of acting roles, demonstrating her impressive range. In *Sphere,* starring Dustin Hoffman, Samuel L. Jackson, and

Sharon Stone, Latifah played a deep-sea diver who helps examine a mysterious glowing sphere. The television miniseries *Mama Flora's Family* was based on a book by *Roots* author Alex Haley. It featured Latifah as the angry and frustrated niece of a family matriarch. In *The Wizard of Oz,* Latifah, playing the Wicked Witch of the West, joined rappers Snoop Doggy Dogg, Heavy D, and others to remake this classic story. But it was her performance as jazz singer Liz Bailey in the acclaimed movie *Living Out Loud,* starring Holly Hunter and Danny DeVito, that most impressed fans and critics. Latifah described her performance as "the best work I've done since *Set It Off.*"

Audiences and reviewers were stunned when Latifah filled movie theaters with a sultry voice so unlike her rap style. Her performance in *Living Out Loud* created an instant following among jazz lovers. One new fan said, "The woman sings with feeling from deep in her soul. The [movie soundtrack] has just become my favorite." Others begged the Queen to do a jazz CD and declared their new respect for the first lady of rap.

While Latifah's acting brought rave reviews, the work left her with little time for her music. Fans began to wonder if they had heard the last from the Queen, who had not released an album in five years. But Latifah had her reasons for holding off. Motown Records was in transition. In six years, the company had three different presidents. Latifah wanted to be sure that these leadership problems were resolved.

When Latifah felt that the time was right, her fourth album, *Order In the Court,* was released in 1998. It was coproduced by Motown and Latifah's own Flavor Unit Records. The album reflected an older, more contemplative Latifah, who mused about life and death in addition to social problems.

Her song "What You Gonna Do" expressed the sadness she still felt about her brother's death. "Life" was a tribute to the slain rappers Tupac Shakur and the

Queen Latifah portrayed a jazz singer in the film Living Out Loud. *Her smooth, sultry voice surprised fans who knew her only as a rap star.*

Notorious B.I.G., who died in separate shooting incidents in 1997. In "Black On Black Love," Latifah hailed the importance of caring for one another.

"It's where I am at this point in my life," Latifah said of her fourth album. "Thinking about love, thinking about life, thinking about God, thinking about beats and rhymes. There is a song that reflects each one of those kind of thoughts or emotions."

Latifah had also reached a point where she wanted to do more to reach women with her message of self-respect, independence, and self-love. Collaborating with *New York Daily News* reporter Karen Hunter, Latifah wrote her autobiography. The book's title comes from her hit single "Ladies First." In January 1999, *Ladies First: Revelations Of A Strong Woman* was published by William Morrow and Company. It featured a touching foreword by Latifah's mother. Latifah embarked on a tour to promote her autobiography and meet the fans who thronged to bookstores. "This book is meant to empower women, to let them know that no matter what you go through, you can overcome it, hold your head high and be a queen," she said.

Latifah shared her positive attributes and accomplishments with readers. But she also wrote about moments in her life that she wasn't proud of, such as using drugs and being arrested for carrying a gun.

Critics applauded Latifah for her honest self-portrait in *Ladies First*. "Latifah delivers her insights with biographical frankness and salty directness that her young female fans are likely to find engaging and convincing," one reviewer wrote. By July 1999, Latifah's life story had reached the number four spot on the Blackboard African-American Bestsellers list of best-selling nonfiction books.

Whether she is writing a book, filming a movie, running her company, or cutting an album, Latifah always makes time to give back to her community. The charitable division of Flavor Unit, the Lancelot H. Owens Foundation, was founded in Winki's memory shortly after his death. It allows her to practice what she preaches.

The foundation provides scholarship money to send minority youths to college. Latifah's friends and coworkers in the entertainment industry help the foundation raise funds for scholarships and other programs. They include a support system of professional mentors, academic and career counselors, and internship placement services. "Flavor Unit employs youths from the inner city who only needed a chance to prove that they could do what they believed in their hearts they could accomplish," Latifah said proudly.

In addition to advocating for inner-city youths, Latifah is a strong supporter of the Women's National Basketball Association and other athletic groups. And when she travels to promote her music and other projects, she takes the time to reach out to others, including sick children and homeless and runaway girls.

"She lets them know she didn't come from a

silver-spoon background, she came from a matriarchal home and we didn't have a lot of money," said Mrs. Owens. "And she was able to overcome and they can too."

When Latifah gives interviews or makes public appearances, she encourages others to give back to their communities. "Come back in the community as a mentor," she tells people. "That's one of the most important things that kids need nowadays. They need someone to talk to who's older but who's not their parent."

At book signings in 1999, Queen Latifah promoted her autobiography, Ladies First.

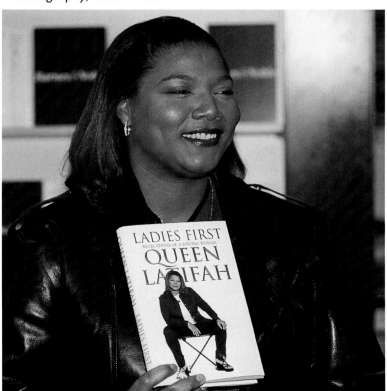

Recently Latifah realized her dream of creating attractive, affordable housing for inner-city New Jersey residents. In yet another company expansion, Latifah created Flavor Unit Real Estate Holdings. She asked her mother to manage the company, which owns a number of residential and commercial properties.

"There are so many buildings around here that are just waiting to be renovated and lived in," Latifah said. "[I want to develop] beautiful low-income housing that looks like townhouses and not projects so people can take pride in them."

Latifah has said she thinks that people need a sense of something to care about. And as a rapper, actor, and businesswoman, she has cared enough to be a positive role model for her fans. Along the way to stardom, she helped other rappers find their place in the spotlight. "Latifah is one of the people who created options for new artists," said Monica Lynch, the Tommy Boy record producer who launched Latifah's recording career.

A b-girl who got her start in a New Jersey 'hood, Latifah continues to inspire men, women, and children across generations and ethnic groups. Editors of *Ladies Home Journal* magazine selected Latifah as one of the most fascinating women of 1998. In the same year, the Professional Women of Color organization honored Latifah for her entrepreneurial spirit and accomplishments. She is ranked number 72 on VH1's list of the "100 Greatest Women of Rock & Roll." Film

Queen Latifah played opposite Denzel Washington in the 1999 movie The Bone Collector.

producers have included her music in such movies as *White Men Can't Jump* and *Girls Town*. Across the country, professors, music reviewers, record producers, and others attend hip-hop conferences where the Queen is often discussed and praised.

While Latifah has achieved a long list of accomplishments in her thirty years, her reign is far from over. She continues to expand Flavor Unit, which has grown to include two more record labels, Jersey Kids and Ghetto Works. And she's working on her fifth album. Although Flavor Unit's three record labels are distributed by large entertainment companies like Warner Brothers, Flavor Unit Records will record and distribute Latifah's fifth album independently so that she can maintain greater control.

Latifah's eleventh movie, *The Bone Collector*, starring Denzel Washington as a paralyzed detective obsessed with catching a serial killer, was released in the fall of 1999. Latifah played a nurse in the movie. Around the same time, the Warner Brothers network helped Latifah take on yet another challenge when it launched a new talk show, *The Queen Latifah Show.*

Latifah is the host and co-executive producer of her own talk show. She reaches audiences with a format of live music and celebrity guests, combined with solution-oriented discussions about social issues. "I come from a unique background, I'm down-to-earth, and people feel like they can talk to me," she said. Latifah's friend and business partner Shakim Compere, who urged Latifah for years to create her own talk show, coproduces the show.

Queen Latifah, left, *and her mother,* right, *spoke to students at the New Jersey Performing Arts Center in Newark in 1999. Latifah remains an inspiration to African American young people.*

While she is adored by millions of fans, Latifah is most comfortable with the people who have supported her throughout her life. With her close friends and relatives, Latifah is free to relax. Her good friends still call her Dana, or sometimes La. She and her mother remain very close. And while Mrs. Owens still teaches at Irvington High School, she is a partner in Flavor Unit Entertainment. Latifah, who often credits her mother with her success, asked Mrs. Owens to share her wisdom by making regular appearances on her talk show. Latifah maintains her relationship with her father as well. She has established close ties to her half siblings Angelo, Michelle, and Kelly.

Running a company and taping *The Queen Latifah Show* five days a week is an intense life. With two staffs working for her—one at Flavor Unit and one for the talk show—Latifah works long hours, often fourteen or more a day. When it's time to relax, she heads to the basketball court and enjoys the company of good friends. She divides her time between New York City, where her talk show is taped, and the New Jersey neighborhoods she still considers home.

The original Flavor Unit members are still part of the Queen's tight posse. It is to herself and these people that she answers. "We are all royalty," Latifah wrote in her autobiography. "Ramsey is my inspiration. Tammy is my conscience. Shakim is my anchor."

Latifah wants to be remembered not as a queen, but for staying true to herself. For years, her friends have helped her stay focused and genuine. Twenty years from now, with her posse still by her side, she hopes she can look back and say, "I stayed in touch with who I was. I didn't sell out. I didn't lose myself. I didn't become someone else just for money. I stayed me. I learned. I grew. And I opened up some doors, or at least showed some other people they can do it, too. I love the idea that there are people who will come after me who will be greater than me."

SOURCES

8   Queen Latifah, *Ladies First* (New York: William Morrow and Co., 1999), 48.
9   Latifah, 58.
10   Tom Gliatto and Sabrina McFarland, "A Hit in *Living Single*, Queen Latifah Mourns the Loss of a Brother," *People*, November 29, 1993, 73.
11   Latifah, xviii.
11   Gliatto and McFarland, 73.
11   Ibid., xii.
12   Ibid., 40.
13   Ibid., 38–39.
15   *Intimate Portrait: Queen Latifah.* Lifetime Productions, Inc.: Peter Leone Productions, 1996, videotape.
15   Latifah, 20.
21   Ibid., 16.
21   Ibid., 17.
22   Ibid., xiv–xv.
23   Ibid., 22.
23   *Intimate Portrait: Queen Latifah.*
26   Latifah, 25.
26   Ibid., 28.
27   Ibid., 30.
30   Ibid., 30.
30   *Intimate Portrait: Queen Latifah.*
30   Ibid.
31   Ibid.
34   Ibid.
34   Laurie Lanzen Harris, ed., "Queen Latifah," in *Biography Today* (Penobscot, MI: Omnigraphics, April 1992), 373.
36   Evelyn C. White, "The Poet And The Rapper," *Essence*, May 22, 1999, 122.
37   Latifah, 69, 70.
37   Ibid., 82
40   Dennis Hunt, "Ten Questions: Queen Latifah," *Los Angeles Times*, September 8, 1991, 54.

40   Harris, 373.

41   Carole Bekane Nagel, ed. *African American Biography* (New York: UXL/Gale Research, 1994), 605.

41   Keith Elliot Greenberg, *Rap* (Minneapolis: Lerner Publications, 1991), 30.

43   Harris, 374.

45   Aldore Collier, "A Royal Rap: Queen Latifah Reigns on and off TV," *Ebony*, December 1993, 116.

45   Latifah, 55.

45-46 Ibid., 53–54.

46   White, 122.

47   Latifah, 48–49.

48   Ibid., 58–59.

49   Ibid., 66.

49   Ibid., 66.

50   Ibid., 64.

50   *Intimate Portrait: Queen Latifah.*

51   Ibid.

51   Ibid.

51   Latifah, 62.

51   "Queen Latifah Says 'There's Life After *Living Single*,'" *Jet*, July 20, 1998, 34.

54   Harris, 373.

54   Latifah, 19.

55   Jae-Ha Kim, "Another Jewel for Her Crown," *Chicago Sun-Times*, January 13, 1999, 47.

55   Hunt, 54.

56   Kent Greene, "Queen Latifah," *Celebrity Biographies,* Baseline II, 1998. Internet source.

57   <http://www.rockonthenet.com/artistsq/ queenlatifah_bio.htm> August 1, 1999.

59   Chris Dafoe, "Rapping Latifah Rules New Tribes," *Toronto Star*, May 18, 1990, D8.

59   Harris, 374.

59   White, 122.

60   Latifah, 68–69.

61   Tricia Rose, *Black Noise: Rap Music and the Black Culture in Contemporary America* (Middleton, CT: Wesleyan University Press, 1994), 165.

61 Karen Schoemer, "Six Nights for Sampling a World of Unsung Bands," *New York Times,* July 13, 1990, C1.
62 Nagel, 607.
63 Bobby Washington, *Who's Hot! Queen Latifah* (New York: Bantam Doubleday Dell, 1992), 39.
63 "What's Hot and What's Not," Gannett News Service, January 17, 1992. News database.
66 Nagel, 605.
    Cameron Barr, "Rap for the Masses," *Christian Science Monitor,* November 4, 1991, 10.
68 Deborah Gregory, "The Queen Rules," *Essence,* October 1993, 57.
68 Business Wire, Inc., "Queen Latifah Goes 'Live' with Flavor Unit West," August 29, 1996. News database.
68 *Intimate Portrait: Queen Latifah.*
69 Harris, 375.
70 Barr, 10.
70 Cheo Hodari Coker, "Queen Latifah Aims to Reign Over Films Too," *Los Angeles Times*, May 20, 1996, F1.
71 <http://www.dosomething.org/build/queen.html>, August 1, 1999.
71 Barr, 10.
74 Latifah, 78.
74 Lynn Elber, "Queen Latifah Fights for Some Self-Satisfaction," *Toronto Sun,* May 19, 1994, 76.
75 Latifah, 88.
76 Ibid., 79.
76 Ibid., 105.
76 *Intimate Portrait: Queen Latifah.*
77 Cindy Pearlman, "Queen Latifa: A Force in Cinema, Music, Television," *Chicago Sun-Times,* October 4, 1998, 3.
79 *Black Reign* liner notes.
81 Monika Guttman, "Queen's Troubled Reign," *USA Weekend,* November 6, 1994, 16.
84 Queen Latifah, "It Changed My Outlook on Life," *USA Weekend,* October 22, 1995, 14.
84 Barbara Ross, "Sobbing Rapper I.D.s Carjack Suspect at Trial," *Daily News,* April 25, 1996, B6.
85 Nagel, 607.

Sources   105

86 *Intimate Portrait: Queen Latifah.*
86 "Queen Latifah Says 'There's Life After *Living Single,'*" 34.
87 Ibid.
87 Jay Lustig and Carrie Stetler, "Latifah is Queen of all she does; Actress, rapper, manager scores in many fields," *Minneaplis Star Tribune,* November 18, 1996, 7E.
87-88 Ibid.
88 Business Wire, Inc.
89 Paula Span, "The Business of Rap as Business: Hip-Hop Stars Are Building Empires," *The Washington Post,* June 4, 1995, G1.
89 Joan Morgan, "The Queen on the Screen," *Essence,* January 1, 1998, 70.
89 "Queen Latifah Says 'There's Life After *Living Single,'*" 34.
92 Donna Freydkin, "When Latifah reigns, she pours it on." CNN Interactive <http://www.cnn.com/SHOWBIZ/music/9809/02/queen.latifah/>, August 8, 1999.
94 "Queen Latifah Says 'There's Life After *Living Single,'*" 34.
94 Kim, 47.
95 *Kirkus Reviews,* December 1, 1998. News database.
95 <http://www.dosomething.org/build/queen.html>, August 1, 1999.
95-96 Ibid.
96 Ibid.
97 Gregory, 57.
97 *Intimate Portrait: Queen Latifah.*
99 Gary Levin, "TV's ChatFest Expanding with Latifah, Short," *USA Today,* January 27, 1999, 1D.
100 Latifah, 75.
101 Pearlman, 3.

SELECTED BIBLIOGRAPHY

BOOKS

Britten, Loretta Y., ed. *African Americans Voice of Triumph: Perseverance.* Alexandria, VA: Time Life Books, 1993.

Guevara, Nancy. "Women Writin' Rappin' Breakin'." *The Year Left 2: An American Socialist Yearbook.* Mike Davis et al., eds. London: Verso, 1987.

Harris, Laurie Lanzen, ed. "Queen Latifah." *Biography Today.* Penobscot, MI: Omnigraphics, April 1992.

Hine, Darlene Clark. *Facts on File Encyclopedia of Black Women in America: Music.* New York: Facts on File, 1997.

Hoobler, Dorothy, and Thomas Hoobler. *Images Across the Ages: African Portraits.* Austin, TX: Steck-Vaughn, 1993.

Hyman, Mark. *Blacks Before America.* Trenton, NJ: Africa World Press, 1994.

Jones, K. Maurice. *Say It Loud: The Story of Rap Music.* Brookfield, CT: Millbrook Press, 1994.

Latifah, Queen. *Ladies First.* New York: William Morrow and Co., 1999.

Nagel, Carole Bekane, ed. *African American Biography.* New York: UXL/Gale Research, 1994.

Stancell, Steven. *Rap Whoz Who: The World of Rap Music.* New York: Schirmer Books, 1996.

ARTICLES

Barr, Cameron. "Rap for the Masses." *Christian Science Monitor,* November 4, 1991.

Collier, Aldore. "A Royal Rap: Queen Latifah Reigns on and off TV." *Ebony,* December 1993.

Dafoe, Chris. "Rapping Latifah Rules New Tribes." *Toronto Star,* May 18, 1990.

Duncan, Amy. "All Hail Queen Latifah's Clever Wordplay." *Christian Science Monitor,* November 22, 1989.

Elber, Lynn. "Queen Latifah Fights for Some Self-Satisfaction." *The Toronto Sun,* May 19, 1994.

"The 50 Most Beautiful People in the World 1999: Queen Latifah Rapper Actress." *People,* May 10, 1999.

Gliatto, Tom, and Sabrina McFarland. "A Hit in *Living Single,* Queen Latifah Mourns the Loss of a Brother." *People,* November 29, 1993.

Gliatto, Tom, and Sabrina McFarland. "Rap of the Town." *People,* May 25, 1992.

Greene, Kent. "Queen Latifah." *Celebrity Biographies.* Baseline II, 1999.

Gregory, Deborah. "The Queen Rules." *Essence,* October 1993.

Guttman, Monika. "Queen's Troubled Reign." *USA Weekend,* November 6, 1994.

Halberstam, Judith. "Starting from Scratch: Female Rappers and Feminist Discourse." *Re-Visions,* Winter 1989.

Hunt, Dennis. "Ten Questions: Queen Latifah." *Los Angeles Times,* September 8, 1991.

Kim, Jae-Ha. "Another Jewel for Her Crown." *Chicago Sun-Times,* January 13, 1999.

Latifah, Queen. "It Changed My Outlook on Life." *USA Weekend,* October 22, 1995.

Maslin, Janet. "Learning About Living, the Hard Way." *New York Times,* November 12, 1993.

Millner, Denene. "Queen Is Her Own Triumvirate: Singing, Acting, Record Business All Ruled by Latifah." *San Diego Union-Tribune,* June 23, 1994.

Mills, David. "Hip-Hop's Rap: Getting Funky and More Feminine." *Washington Post,* November 18, 1990.

Moon, Tom. "Rapping Out a Woman's Point of View; New Rhymes and Rhythms Answer Macho Messages." *Bergen County Record,* March 10, 1991.

Moon, Tom. "A Reluctant Role Model." *Calgary Herald,* October 20, 1991.

Moore, Teresa. "Queen Latifah Expands Her Empire." *San Francisco Chronicle,* January 31, 1999.

Morgan, Joan. "The Queen on the Screen." *Essence,* January 1, 1998.

Moton, Tony. "Another Gem in Her Crown." *Omaha World-Herald,* November 6, 1998.

Norment, Lynn. "Queen Latifah." *Ebony,* November 1999.

Pearlman, Cindy. "Queen Latifah: A Force in Cinema, Music, Television." *Chicago Sun-Times,* October 4, 1998.

"Queen Latifah Says 'There's Life After *Living Single.*'" *Jet,* July 20, 1998.

Span, Paula. "The Business of Rap as Business: Hip-Hop Stars Are Building Empires." *Washington Post,* June 4, 1995.

Watrous, Peter. "When the Queen Speaks, People Listen." *New York Times,* August 21, 1991.

White, Evelyn C. "The Poet And The Rapper." *Essence,* May 22, 1999.

Wiltz, Terea. "The Rap on the Queen: It's Been the Best and Worst of Years for Queen Latifah." *St. Louis Post-Dispatch,* September 13, 1996.

VIDEOS/TELEVISION

Before They Were Rock Stars. VH1, May 1, 1999.

Intimate Portrait: Queen Latifah. Lifetime Productions, Inc.: Peter Leone Productions, 1996.

WEBSITES

Africana.com
<http://www.africana.com>

The Black Market
<http://www.theblackmarket.com>

BlackVoices
<http://www.blackvoices.com>

Flavor Unit Entertainment
<http://www.flavorunitent.com>

Kolorscope, Inc.
<http://www.kolorscope.com>

MTV News
<http://mtv.com/news>

Polygram Records
<http://www.polygram-us.com>

Professional Women of Color
<http://www.pwconline.org>

Rap, Race & Equality
<http://www.rapmusic.nu>

Rock on the Net
<http:www.rockonthenet.com>

Rock the Vote
<http://www.rockthevote.org>

Urban Showcase
<http://www.music.com/showcase/urban/>

DISCOGRAPHY

All Hail The Queen 1989
Nature Of A Sista 1991

Black Reign 1993
Order In The Court 1998

FILMOGRAPHY

House Party 2 1991
Jungle Fever 1991
Juice 1992
My Life 1993
Set It Off 1996
Hoodlum 1997

Living Out Loud 1998
*Mama Flora's Family, Parts 1
   & 2* 1998
Sphere 1998
The Wizard of Oz 1998
The Bone Collector 1999

INDEX

OTHER TITLES FROM LERNER AND A&E®:

ABOUT THE AUTHOR

Amy Ruth lives in Williamsburg, Virginia, with her husband, writer Jim Meisner Jr. This is her fourth book in the BIOGRAPHY® series.

PHOTO ACKNOWLEDGMENTS

© Walter Weissman/Globe Photos, Inc., pp. 2, 96; © Bettmann/Corbis, pp. 6, 16, 19; © Jay Blakesberg/Retna Ltd., p. 9; State Museum, Berlin, p. 14; Newark Public Library, p. 24; Globe Photos, Inc., pp. 32, 36; © Andrea Renault/Globe Photos, Inc., p. 35; © Chuck Pulin/Star File, p. 38 (top); © Glen E. Friedman/Rush Productions, p. 38 (bottom); © John Bellissimo/Corbis, p. 39; ©Al Pereira/Star File, pp. 41, 42, 64; Hollywood Book and Poster, p. 46, 93; © Laura Levine/Rush Productions, p. 47; © Bob Gruen/Star File, p. 50; © Todd Kaplan/Star File, p. 52; © Corbis, p. 54; © Gene Shaw/Star File, p. 57; © Ernie Paniccioli/Retna Ltd., p. 58; Tommy Boy Records, p. 62; Jive Records, p. 67; © Fitzroy Barrett/Globe Photos, Inc., p. 69; © Bill Davila/Retna Ltd., p. 72; Photofest, p. 78; © Lisa Rose/Globe Photos, Inc., pp. 81, 90; © Kwame Brathwaite/Globe Photos, Inc., p. 88; © Takashi Seida/Photofest, p. 98; AP/Wide World Photos, p. 99; © Cheryl Himmelstein/Retna Ltd., p. 101.

Front cover: © Steve Granitz/Retna Ltd.
Back cover: © Sandra Johnson/Retna Ltd.